Small Talk

To Carl & Emma,
   Hope you'll be able to add a
few choice quotes of your own over
the years!
   Lots of love, Maureen & Bill xxx.

For Sarah and Emma, with my love

3 5 7 9 10 8 6 4

Originally published as *To You with Love* in 1999 by Ebury Press
This revised and updated edition first published in 2004 by Ebury Press /
Random House · 20 Vauxhall Bridge Road · London SW1V 2SA

Random House Australia (Pty) Limited
20 Alfred Street · Milsons Point · Sydney · New South Wales 2061 · Australia

Random House New Zealand Limited
18 Poland Road · Glenfield · Auckland 10 · New Zealand

Random House South Africa (Pty) Ltd
Endulini · 5A Jubilee Road · Parktown 2193 · South Africa

Random House UK Limited Reg. No. 954009

www. randomhouse.co.uk

A CIP catalogue record for this book is available from the British Library

ISBN: 0 09 189113 2

Papers used by Ebury Press are natural, recyclable products made from wood
grown in sustainable forests.

Printed and bound in Denmark by Nørhaven Paperback, Viborg

Small Talk

NANETTE NEWMAN

EBURY PRESS
LONDON

Foreword

Like most mothers, when my daughters, Sarah and Emma, were growing up I was often amused by what they said, and sometimes surprised by the perception and logic of the things they came out with. It was this that made me decide to gather together childrens' sayings and drawings from family and friends and then, spreading the net wider, enlisting the help of schools and hospitals.

Very soon material poured in from everywhere and I came to the conclusion that there must be many people like me who not only love the sophisticated, cynical and senduppish style of humour, but

Nanette by Elizabeth

Nanette by Chris

also enjoy the very different type of humour that comes from a small child. In their innocence, the very young often get right to the heart of the matter.

Now, with five grandchildren, I realise how lucky I am not to have lost touch with that enchanting time in a child's life when they say it like it is – and 'saying it like it is' proves worth listening to.

I hope you enjoy this collection.

Nanette Newman

Nanette by Alice   **Nanette by Emma**

Love and Marriage

its apity you have to
fall in love with boys because
they allways pinch you

Beryl aged 7

I saw a book once with all drawings on it about falling in love and I think you have to have eggs.

Vera aged 5

you should never love someone
you dont like much

Katy aged 7

To get married you have to shave you're legs. I think

Alice aged 5

My Granddad says he doesnt
like women So we bought
Him a cat

Robert aged 8

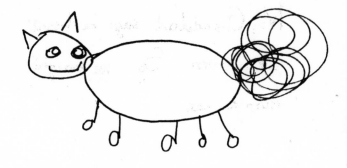

I wouldn't fall in love because girls are all spotty and they wisper

Norman aged 6

You must take care
of Love — if You
Don't it goes bad

James aged 5

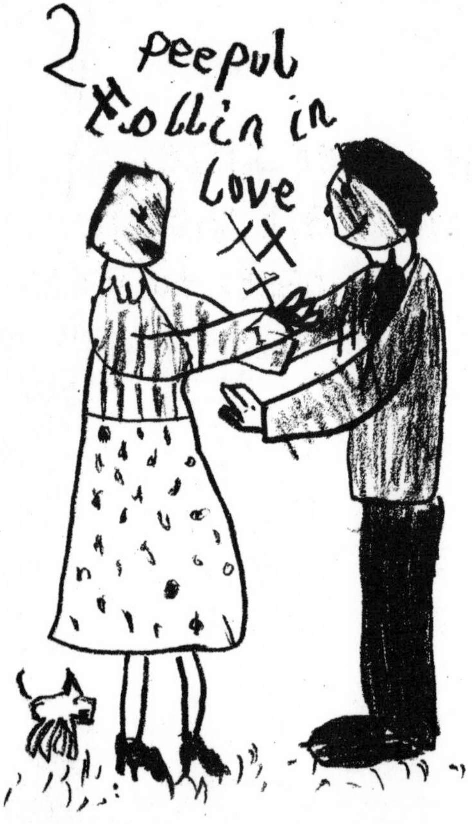
2 peepul follin in love
XX
X

My sister Kisses her boy friend all the time its very nasty to watch

James aged 6

when I get married
I'll have a cake like
snow white and we'll
play pass the parcel

Olivia aged 5

when you marry a girl you have to give her a best man

Richard aged 7

They throw rice
pudding at you
when you get
married

Anya aged 5

A wedding

I don't know why my uncle wanted an awful wedded wife

Laurie aged 7

my dad was going to marry
my mum but he forgot

Nick aged 6

I am helping my
Mummy choose my
next Daddy.

Anna aged 5

My mother said she
won't get maried again
it's too much truble

Shirley aged 5

my dad has found
a better mummy for
us than the last one

Michael aged 6

Babies

I nearly know how to have babies but we don't do it till next term

Frances aged 7

If you dount want babies you should practice contradiction

Lynn aged 9

The man next door has a
baby in his tummy but it
never comes out

Janet aged 6

if you put a man and a
woman in bed together
one of them will have a baby

Paul aged 9

when you're pregnant you become
sicker and fatter and nastier
every day

Marianne aged 9

To have a baby you have to make love to someone who doesn't mind

Marianne aged 9

BabyS
Dont
grow
On Trees

If you dont want to have a baby you have to wear a safety belt

Alison aged 5

Once you've had a baby
you cant put it back.

Andrea aged 6

Babies come out of your tummy
on a piece of string.

Graham aged 7

A baby comes out of the mummy tummy and bites the Doctor. and the Docor Smacks it.

Edward aged 6

IF a baby drops out of your tummy when your shopping You must ring the police.

Deborah aged 6

A new borned baby can't
talk it just thinks all day

Tina aged 6

Babies cry in the Dark becorse they think they havnt been born yet.

Lorri aged 6

you have to Love
your loaby brother
otherwise ne geos wind

Alice aged 4

Babies are'nt Very useful

Brian aged 6

Babees need to be loved by their mother in case evrybody hates them when they grow up.

Norman aged 7

If you don't love your baby it won't come and visit you when your old

Noura aged 7

My brother was born even though I didnt want him.

Noel aged 6

my mummy let me hold my brother when he was born and I didn't drop him once

Serena aged 8

you should never squeeze a
baby when its new because
its head isn't set yet

Charles aged 6

My Auntys baby jumped
out of her tummy
when she wasn't looking,
and she hadn't bought
the cot yet

Isabelle aged 6

Mum had twins my
brother went up
to heaven but
I stayed here

Joshua aged 6

Family

my mother has witigh
yelleow hare. pinkish
eyes and lots of Teeth
and she Is very
brtifvll.

Anna aged 6

My uncle has
started to grow to
Look Like a mouse.

Simon aged 5

something that
makes me sad

mummy went away even though I loved her.

Michael aged 6

auntie iris came all the
way from Skegness

Steven aged 6

I was adopted so my

parents wanted me

very badly,

Lydia aged 8

I am thankful to God
for making me only one
brother and not making
me have two

Elizabeth aged 9

I want to Swop my Sister
for Somethiing better.

Alex aged 4

If my Sister Keeps on looking in the mirrer she'll Turn into a Vanity

Susan aged 6

My sister carnt reed or rite and shes a literat

Paula aged 8

We went to peter Pan
and I hoped that Tinkerbell

Would die because shes
like my sister.

Guy aged 6

we are going to
windsor Castle to see the
Queen's private parts

Becky aged 7

Bananas are the
best fruit because
you can undress them

Yasmin aged 5

I went on holiday to
Brocolli last year

Sally aged 5

pets

True love is when some thing
has died and you still remember it
like my hamster.

Bobby aged 6

My rabbit is the saddest person I know.

Carlo aged 8

I would like to marry my dog.
but it isint alowed, is it?

Bruce aged 6

Guinea Pigs Like
Peace

Emma aged 4

Goldfish are sex maniaks mainiaks

Shaun aged 9

You can't teach a
goldfish anything
they're too lazy

Yasmin aged 6

A ladybrd is
a very cheep pet

Hugo aged 6

My hamster went to heaven and came back a different colour.

Marilyn aged 6

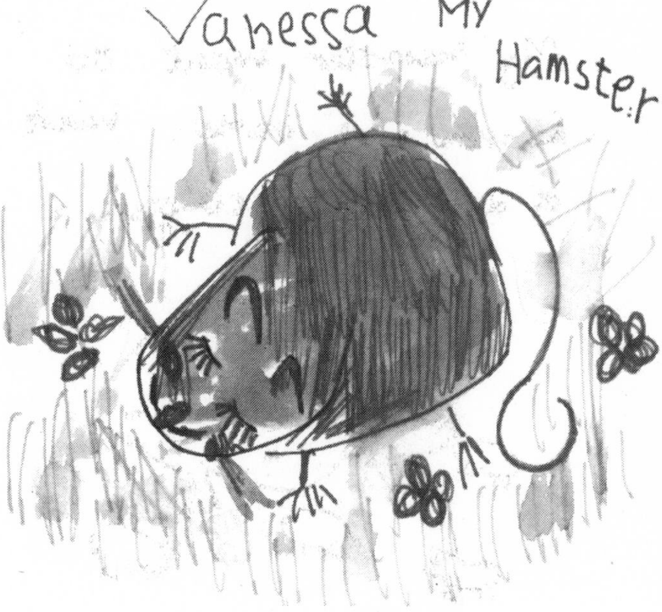
Vanessa My Hamster

My rabit was very sorri
to di becorse he likked
eeting

Rushka aged 5

I think rabbits make very good mothers

Sara aged 6

My rabbit was a ~~be~~ bachelor.

David aged 5

I had a baby budgie called Tabatha but she died before she knew what she was.

Ruth aged 8

My dog wants to give
all dogs he meets babies.
Nes a terrible responsiblity

Albert aged 7

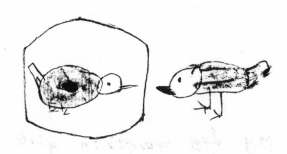

My budgie broke is neck.
it served him rite
because he was always
kissing himself in the
mirrer.

Tim aged 6

School

when I am at school my
mummy
h az fun

Stephen aged 5

My mummy cried on my first day at school so I had to take her home.

Penny aged 5

My Teecher is very crule.
she smaks Peple all day
and she eats f rogs legs
and maks cros spells.
I dont li Ke her becos
she says I tell fibs.

David aged 6

I love my daddy becorse he give me a good ejukashun

Zoe aged 6

MY MUMMY GOZE
To A SPEEZKOL
FOR HAVING
& babis

my mummy goze
TO A skool for
Having babis

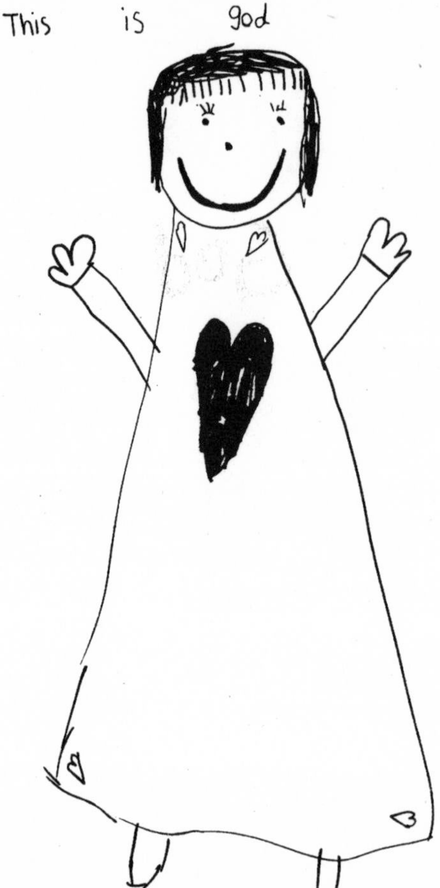
This is god

God

People keep their eyes open when they pray in case Jesus arrives

Adam aged 7

god loves everyone who is good
like me and my friend lucy but
not peopul like gillian who takes
other peoples rubbers

Katy aged 6

my sister is always
writing to jesus an he
sends her chociates an
once he sent her two
lots of chociates on the
same day but she won't
tell me where to write.

Ian aged 6

I saw Jesus in the supermarket once. He was giving away soap powders

Lynne aged 6

Jesus had a cow and a donkey but I think he would rather have had a hamster.

Brent aged 6

I say my prayers with my eyes open so I can hear what I am saying.

Robin aged 5

If you eat sweets in church the vicar tells Jesus

Robert aged 5

My granny always talks to
Jesus on Sundays. The
rest of the week she goes
to Bingo which is where he
lives sometimes.

Charles aged 5

They told me to bow to the
Alter but he wasnt there.
I think he'd gone out with
the vicar.

Emma aged 7

at harvest festival God
comes down and eats all
the Food in the church

Melanie aged 5

I think the Pope must have been a good baby

Elizabeth aged 6

Nuns have neck laces which they fiddle about with in church

Darin aged 8

The animals went into the Ark
two by two but they came out lots
and lots becuase they had some
baby's during the week

Jane aged 6

I think Jesus was black like me

Hamen aged 7

vicars can say Jesus Christ
but if I say it
I get a smack

Luke aged 6

Christmas

In our school Nativity play,
Joseph got chickenpox and
spoilt it

Amanda aged 7

Mary and her husband tried to get a room at the Holiday Inn but it was full

Mark aged 7

If you are Jewish you
don't have christmas you
have a harmonica instead

Edward aged 6

Joseeph's wife Mary had an immaculate contraption

Cathy aged 7

Father Christmas and Jesus are best friends

Darryl aged 7

We are doing an activity play this Christmas, it's about how Jesus was bored

Melanie aged 5

Nobody covered Jesus
up when he was born,
he could have caught flu

Sidney aged 5

I don't know how the King got FRANKENSTEIN into the box

Daniel aged 6

people keep starring
at baby Jesus
because mary really
wanted a girl

Kirsten aged 6

Jesus was born with a yellow frill round his head like his Mother

Jeffrey aged 5

war and peace

Peace

My mummy and daddy like
Peace.

They dont often get it.

David aged 7

when people start
wars they never
Know how to Stop.

Alanda aged 6

I think war is exciting on television for real I think It is horrible

John aged 7